The Meaning of Surah 54 Al-Qamar The Moon (La Luna) From The Holy Quran Bilingual Edition English Spanish

Jannah Firdaus Mediapro

Published by Jannah Firdaus Mediapro Studio, 2021.

While every precaution has been taken in the preparation of this book, the publisher assumes no responsibility for errors or omissions, or for damages resulting from the use of the information contained herein.

THE MEANING OF SURAH 54 AL-QAMAR THE MOON (LA LUNA) FROM THE HOLY QURAN BILINGUAL EDITION ENGLISH SPANISH

First edition. January 19, 2021.

Copyright © 2021 Jannah Firdaus Mediapro.

Written by Jannah Firdaus Mediapro.

Prologue

The Meaning of Surah 54 Al-Qamar The Moon (La Luna) From The Holy Quran Bilingual Edition English and Spanish.

The Surah revolves around the Signs of Allah SWT (God) and those who belie and deny them from amongst the polytheists. The splitting of the Qamar [moon] is amongst the great signs shown by God to the people of Makkah which they still resulted on them continuing their disbelief.

The Surah talks about the approaching Day of Judgment. It describes some of the scenes of that Day. It also tells us that Allah's judgment may come here and now. There are references to the flood that came at the time of Prophet Noah AS, the punishment of the people of 'Ad, Thamud, People of Prophet Lot AS, the Pharaoh and his people. It ends with the good news for the Believers who will be near their Lord in the gardens of bliss. This Surah takes its name from the first Ayat:

"The Hour has come near, and the moon has split [in two]." (54:1).

Surah al-Qamar is in the 27th Juzz and the word Qamar [moon] appears in the Qur'an 27 times. An interesting observation is that the Moon orbits the Earth every 27 days. There are 55 Ayat in this Surah.

In this Surah the disbelievers of Makkah have been warned for their stubbornness which they had adopted against the invitation of the Prophet. The amazing and wonderful phenomenon of the splitting of the Moon was a manifest sign of the truth that the Resurrection, of which the Prophet was giving them the news, could take place and that it had approached near at hand. The great sphere of the Moon had split into two distinct parts in front of their very eyes. The two parts had separated and receded so much apart from each other that to the onlookers one part had appeared on one side of the mountain and the other on the other side of it. Then, in an instant the two had rejoined.

This was a manifest proof of the truth that the system of the Universe was neither eternal nor immortal, it could be disrupted. Huge stars and planets could split asunder, disintegrate, collide with each other, and everything that had been depicted in the Qur'an in connection with the description of the details of Resurrection, could happen. Not only this: it was also a portent that the disintegration of the system of the Universe had begun and the time was near when Resurrection would take place. The Prophet invited the people's attention to this event only with this object in view and asked them to mark it and be a witness to it. But the disbelievers described it as a magical illusion and persisted in their denial. For this stubbornness they have been reproached in this Surah.

La sura gira en torno a los signos de Allah SWT (Dios) y aquellos que los desmienten y niegan entre los politeístas. La división de Qamar [luna] es una de las grandes señales mostradas por Dios a la gente de La Meca, que todavía resultaron en que continuaran con su incredulidad.

La sura habla del próximo Día del Juicio. Describe algunas de las escenas de ese día. También nos dice que el juicio de Allah puede venir aquí y ahora. Hay referencias al diluvio que vino en la época del profeta Noé AS, el castigo del pueblo de 'Ad, Thamud, el pueblo del profeta Lot AS, el faraón y su pueblo. Termina con las buenas nuevas para los creyentes que estarán cerca de su Señor en los jardines de la dicha. Esta Surah toma su nombre del primer Ayat:

"La Hora se ha acercado, y la luna se ha partido [en dos]". (54: 1)

Surah al-Qamar está en el 27 de Juzz y la palabra Qamar [luna] aparece en el Corán 27 veces. Una observación interesante es que la Luna orbita la Tierra cada 27 días. Hay 55 Ayat en esta Sura.

THE MEANING OF SURAH 54 AL-QAMAR THE MOON FROM THE HOLY QURAN BILINGUAL EDITION ENGLISH SPANISH

En esta Sura, los incrédulos de La Meca han sido advertidos por su terquedad que habían adoptado contra la invitación del Profeta. El asombroso y maravilloso fenómeno de la división de la Luna fue un signo manifiesto de la verdad de que la Resurrección, de la que el Profeta les estaba dando la noticia, podía tener lugar y que se había acercado muy cerca. La gran esfera de la Luna se había dividido en dos partes distintas frente a sus propios ojos. Las dos partes se habían separado y retrocedido tanto entre sí que para los espectadores una parte había aparecido en un lado de la montaña y la otra en el otro lado. Luego, en un instante, los dos se habían reunido.

Esta fue una prueba manifiesta de la verdad de que el sistema del Universo no era ni eterno ni inmortal, podría romperse. Enormes estrellas y planetas podrían dividirse, desintegrarse, colisionar entre sí, y podría suceder todo lo que se había descrito en el Corán en relación con la descripción de los detalles de la Resurrección. No solo esto: también era un presagio de que la desintegración del sistema del Universo había comenzado y se acercaba el momento en que tendría lugar la Resurrección.

El Profeta llamó la atención de la gente sobre este evento solo con este objeto a la vista y les pidió que lo marcaran y fueran testigos de él. Pero los incrédulos lo describieron como una ilusión mágica y persistieron en su negación. Por esta terquedad se les ha reprochado en esta Surah.

Chapter 1 Surah 54 Al-Qamar The Moon (La Luna) Arabic Version

1. IQTARABATI ALSSAA'ATU wainsyaqqa alqamaru

2. wa-in yaraw aayatan yu'ridhuu wayaquuluu sihrun mustamirrun

3. wakadzdzabuu waittaba'uu ahwaa-ahum wakullu amrin mustaqirrun

4. walaqad jaa-ahum mina al-anbaa-i maa fiihi muzdajarun

5. hikmatun baalighatun famaa tughnii alnnudzuru

6. fatawalla 'anhum yawma yad'u alddaa'i ilaa syay-in nukurin

7. khusysya'an abshaaruhum yakhrujuuna mina al-ajdaatsi ka-annahum jaraadun muntasyirun

8. muhthi'iina ilaa alddaa'i yaquulu alkaafiruuna haadzaa yawmun 'asirun

9. kadzdzabat qablahum qawmu nuuhin fakadzdzabuu 'abdanaa waqaaluu majnuunun waizdujira

10. fada'aa rabbahu annii maghluubun faintashir

11. fafatahnaa abwaaba alssamaa-i bimaa-in munhamirin

12. wafajjarnaa al-ardha 'uyuunan failtaqaa almaau 'alaa amrin qad qudira

13. wahamalnaahu 'alaa dzaati alwaahin wadusurin

14. tajrii bi-a'yuninaa jazaa-an liman kaana kufira

15. walaqad taraknaahaa aayatan fahal min muddakirin

16. fakayfa kaana 'adzaabii wanudzuri

17. walaqad yassarnaa alqur-aana lildzdzikri fahal min muddakirin

18. kadzdzabat 'aadun fakayfa kaana 'adzaabii wanudzuri

19. innaa arsalnaa 'alayhim riihan sharsharan fii yawmi nahsin mustamirrin

20. tanzi'u alnnaasa ka-annahum a'jaazu nakhlin munqa'irin

21. fakayfa kaana 'adzaabii wanudzuri

22. walaqad yassarnaa alqur-aana lildzdzikri fahal min muddakirin

23. kadzdzabat tsamuudu bialnnudzuri

24. faqaaluu abasyaran minnaa waahidan nattabi'uhu innaa idzan lafii dhalaalin wasu'urin

25. aulqiya aldzdzikru 'alayhi min bayninaa bal huwa kadzdzaabun asyirun

26. saya'lamuuna ghadan mani alkadzdzaabu al-asyiru

27. innaa mursiluu alnnaaqati fitnatan lahum fairtaqibhum waisthabir

28. wanabbi/hum anna almaa-a qismatun baynahum kullu syirbin muhtadharun

29. fanaadaw shaahibahum fata'aataa fa'aqara

30. fakayfa kaana 'adzaabii wanudzuri

31. innaa arsalnaa 'alayhim shayhatan waahidatan fakaanuu kahasyiimi almuhtazhiri

32. walaqad yassarnaa alqur-aana lildzdzikri fahal min muddakirin

33. kadzdzabat qawmu luuthin bialnnudzuri

34. innaa arsalnaa 'alayhim hasiban illaa aala luuthin na-jjaynaahum bisaharin

35. ni'matan min 'indinaa kadzaalika najzii man syakara

36. walaqad andzarahum bathsyatanaa fatamaaraw bialnnudzuri

37. walaqad raawaduuhu 'an dhayfihi fathamasnaa a'yu-nahum fadzuuquu 'adzaabii wanudzuri

38. walaqad shabbahahum bukratan 'adzaabun mus-taqirrun

39. fadzuuquu 'adzaabii wanudzuri

40. walaqad yassarnaa alqur-aana lildzdzikri fahal min muddakirin

41. walaqad jaa-a aala fir'awna alnnudzuru

42. kadzdzabuu bi-aayaatinaa kullihaa fa-akhadznaahum akhdza 'aziizin muqtadirin

43. akuffaarukum khayrun min ulaa-ikum am lakum baraa-atun fii alzzuburi

44. am yaquuluuna nahnu jamii'un muntashirun

45. sayuhzamu aljam'u wayuwalluuna alddubura

46. bali alssaa'atu maw'iduhum waalssaa'atu adhaa wa-amarru

47. inna almujrimiina fii dhalaalin wasu'urin

48. yawma yushabuuna fii alnnaari 'alaa wujuuhihim dzuuquu massa saqara

49. innaa kulla syay-in khalaqnaahu biqadarin

50. wamaa amrunaa illaa waahidatun kalamhin bial-bashari

51. walaqad ahlaknaa asyyaa'akum fahal min muddakirin

---

52. wakullu syay-in fa'aluuhu fii alzzuburi

---

53. wakullu shaghiirin wakabiirin mustatharun

---

54. inna almuttaqiina fii jannaatin wanaharin

---

55. fii maq'adi shidqin 'inda maliikin muqtadirin

Chapter 2 The Translation of Surah 54 Al-Qamar The Moon (La Luna) English Version

1. The Hour has drawn near, and the moon has been cleft asunder (the people of Makkah requested Prophet Muhammad ﷺ to show them a miracle, so he showed them the splitting of the moon).

2. And if they see a sign, they turn away, and say: "This is continuous magic."

3. They belied (the Verses of Allah, this Qur'an), and followed their own lusts. And every matter will be settled [according to the kind of deeds (for the doer of good deeds, his deeds will take him to Paradise, and similarly evil deeds will take their doers to Hell)].

4. And indeed there has come to them news (in this Qur'an) wherein there is (enough warning) to check (them from evil),

5. Perfect wisdom (this Qur'an), but (the preaching of) warners benefit them not,

6. So (O Muhammad ﷺ) withdraw from them. The Day that the caller will call (them) to a terrible thing.

7. They will come forth, with humbled eyes from (their) graves as if they were locusts spread abroad,

8. Hastening towards the caller, the disbelievers will say: "This is a hard Day."

9. The people of Nuh (Noah) denied (their Messenger) before them, they rejected Our slave, and said: "A madman!" and he was insolently rebuked and threatened.

10. Then he invoked his Lord (saying): "I have been overcome, so help (me)!"

11. So We opened the gates of heaven with water pouring forth.

12. And We caused the earth to gush forth with springs. So the waters (of the heaven and the earth) met for a matter predestined.

13. And We carried him on a (ship) made of planks and nails,

14. Floating under Our Eyes, a reward for him who had been rejected!

15. And indeed, We have left this as a sign, then is there any that will remember (or receive admonition)?

16. Then how (terrible) was My Torment and My Warnings?

17. And We have indeed made the Qur'an easy to understand and remember, then is there any that will remember (or receive admonition)?

18. 'Ad (people) belied (their Prophet, Hud), then how (terrible) was My Torment and My Warnings?

19. Verily, We sent against them a furious wind of harsh voice on a day of evil omen and continuous calamity.

20. Plucking out men as if they were uprooted stems of date-palms.

21. Then, how (terrible) was My Torment and My Warnings?

22. And We have indeed made the Qur'an easy to understand and remember, then is there any that will remember (or receive admonition)?

23. Thamud (people also) belied the warnings.

24. For they said: "A man! Alone from among us, that we are to follow? Truly, then we should be in error and distress or madness!"

25. "Is it that the Reminder is sent to him [Prophet Salih (Saleh)] alone from among us? Nay, he is an insolent liar!"

26. Tomorrow they will come to know, who is the liar, the insolent one!

27. Verily, We are sending the she-camel as a test for them. So watch them [O Salih (Saleh)], and be patient!

28. And inform them that the water is to be shared between (her and) them. Each one's right to drink being established (by turns).

29. But they called their comrade and he took (a sword) and killed (her).

30. Then, how (terrible) was My Torment and My Warnings?

31. Verily, We sent against them a single *Saihah* (torment – awful cry, etc.), and they became like the dry stubble of a fold-builder.

32. And indeed, We have made the Qur'an easy to understand and remember, then is there any that will remember (or receive admonition)?

33. The people of Lout (Lot) belied the warnings.

34. Verily, We sent against them a violent storm of stones (which destroyed them all), except the family of Lout (Lot), whom We saved in last hour of the night,

35. As a Favour from Us, thus do We reward him who gives thanks (by obeying Us).

36. And he [Lout (Lot)] indeed had warned them of Our Grasp, but they did doubt the warnings!

37. And they indeed sought to shame his guest (by asking to commit sodomy with them). So We blinded their eyes, "Then taste you My Torment and My Warnings."

38. And verily, an abiding torment seized them early in the morning.

39. "Then taste you My Torment and My Warnings."

40. And indeed, We have made the Qur'an easy to understand and remember, then is there any that will remember (or receive admonition)?

41. And indeed, warnings came to the people of Fir'aun (Pharaoh) [through Musa (Moses) and Harun (Aaron)].

42. (They) belied all Our Signs, so We seized them with a Seizure of the All-Mighty, All-Capable to carry out what he Will (Omnipotent).

43. Are your disbelievers (O Quraish!) better than these [nations of Nuh (Noah), Lout (Lot), Salih (Saleh), and the people of Fir'aun (Pharaoh), etc., who were de-

stroyed)? Or have you an immunity (against Our Tor-ment) in the Divine Scriptures?

44. Or do they say: "We are a great multitude, and we shall be victorious.?"

45. Their multitude will be put to flight, and they will show their backs.

46. Nay, but the Hour is their appointed time (for their full recompense), and the Hour will be more grievous and more bitter.

47. Verily, the *Mujrimun* (polytheists, disbelievers, sinners, criminals, etc.) are in error (in this world) and will burn (in the Hell-fire in the Hereafter).

48. The Day they will be dragged in the Fire on their faces (it will be said to them): "Taste you the touch of Hell!"

49. Verily, We have created all things with *Qadar* (Divine Preordainments of all things before their creation, as written in the Book of Decrees *Al-Lauh Al-Mahfuz*).

50. And Our Commandment is but one, as the twinkling of an eye.

51. And indeed, We have destroyed your likes, then is there any that will remember (or receive admonition)?

52. And each and everything they have done is noted in (their) Records (of deeds).

53. And everything, small and big is written (in *Al-Lauh Al-Mahfuz* already beforehand. before it befalls, or is done by its doer) (See the Qur'an V.57:22).

54. Verily, The *Muttaqun* (pious), will be in the midst of Gardens and Rivers (Paradise).

55. In a seat of truth (Paradise), near the Omnipotent King (Allah, the All-Blessed, the Most High, the Owner of Majesty and Honour).

Chapter 3 The Meaning of Surah 54 Al-Qamar The Moon (La Luna)

English Version

VERSES 1-8 THE DAY of Resurrection and the heedlessness of the polytheists

When Prophet Muhammad delivered the message of God to the people of Mecca, most of them strongly rejected the concept of resurrection. They refused to accept him as being the Messenger of God and demanded that if this world is really going to come to an end then there should be some physical sign, some miracle that should be shown to them as a proof. So five years before the Hijrah (migration) of the Prophet to Madina, God made them witness a miracle. One night they saw the moon split into two pieces and the two halves were so separated that each one appeared on either side of the mount Hira.

After a moment the moon was again joined together. One would think that after seeing such a tremendous sign, they would have accepted the truth, but it did not affect their attitude at all. They stubbornly said that it was just some kind of magic and nothing else. Why do people persist in remaining ignorant of the truth? Why don't they accept such clear proofs? It is because their lives revolve around their own desires and their false self-image makes it almost impossible for them to admit that they were chasing the wrong ideals. Therefore, they prefer to ignore all those things that make them uncomfortably aware of the truth.

The splitting of the moon was not the only sign of God's power; rather, the people of Mecca were also well informed about the nations that had been destroyed before them, because of rejecting God's message that the Prophets had brought to them.

God has given us the choice to think and choose our way of life in this world but those who misuse this choice, and reject God's guidance should not forget that there would come a day when they will not be able to say "no" to the caller, who will call them towards the final Judgement. The arrogant speeches and arguments against God and His Prophet will all be forgotten and they will rush blindly towards their fate.

Verses 9-42 Evil was the end of the preceding nations that belied their Messengers

The people of Noah were so arrogant that they forgot their own helplessness. God sent upon them a mighty flood which drowned everything except the boat carrying Prophet Noah and the few people who had believed in God. This shows God's extreme mercy and compassion for His Messenger and for the believers of truth, but at the same time His punishment for those who stubbornly reject His message, is also evident.

People of 'Ad were extremely powerful, not only in skills but also in physical attributes; but when they continually rejected the message of God, He sent to them a severely cold wind which gave them a humiliating punishment. Then the people of Thamud also made the same error. They were also very proud of their worldly success, and thought that Prophet Salih was just spreading some self-created stories or lies. Then they demanded a miracle and God sent to them a she-camel, about which they had been warned not to give her any harm, but they killed it thinking that they could get away with whatever they desired. Consequently, God gave them a painful end.

The people of Lot were the first people to indulge in homosexuality, and it had blinded their senses to such an extent that when the angels came to the Prophet's house in the guise of young men, these people rushed to have them; nothing mattered to them except the fulfilment of their lust.

The same thing happened to Pharaoh, when he thought himself to be indestructible.

A common misunderstanding is that the Quran is for scholars. God is saying in such clear words that He has Himself made it easy for us to understand and now it's up to us to contemplate and receive its guidance. This is the only book in the world which has been read by all sorts of people. Even illiterate people can benefit from its clear guidance. Along with simplicity, there is an amazing depth in its words that stimulates the intellect of highly learned people too.

Verses 43-55 Threatening the polytheists and giving glad tidings to the pious

How can they delude themselves when God has sent such clear warnings? Those who persist in their disbelief and do not bother to read the Quran or follow the teachings of Prophet Muhammad, should know that they are committing a terrible crime, even if they are in an illusion of being "good people."

In this world, they made fun of the believers that they were being overly concerned with the torment of Hell. Their claim is that God is so merciful that He cannot burn anyone, but God is warning them that this fire will definitely touch those who made fun of it and made no effort to save their souls from it.

At the end of this chapter, God is showing us a glimpse of the splendid gardens of delight, the beautiful Paradise, which He has prepared so lovingly for the ones who remained faithful to Him in the worldly life. These people willingly sacrificed their egos and desires for the sake of God so He will give them this wonderful reward where all their desires will be fulfilled eternally.

Chapter 4 The Translation of Surah 54 Al-Qamar The Moon (La Luna) Spanish Version

1.La Hora se ha acercado y la luna se ha dividido en dos (la gente de La Meca pidió al Profeta Muhammadﷺ para mostrarles un milagro, entonces les mostró la división de la luna).

2.Y si ven una señal, se vuelven y dicen: "Esto es magia continua".

3.Desmintieron (los Versos de Allah, este Corán) y siguieron sus propios deseos. Y todo asunto será resuelto [de acuerdo con el tipo de hechos (para el hacedor de buenas obras, sus obras lo llevarán al Paraíso, y de manera similar las malas acciones llevarán a sus hacedores al Infierno)].

4.Y, de hecho, les ha llegado noticias (en este Corán) en las que hay (advertencia suficiente) para detenerlos (del mal),

5.Perfecta sabiduría (este Qur'an), pero (la predicación de) los advertidores no los beneficia,

6.Entonces (Oh Muhammadﷺ) retirarse de ellos. El día en que la persona que llama los llamará para algo terrible.

7.Saldrán de sus tumbas con ojos humillados, como langostas esparcidas por todas partes,

8.Apresurándose hacia la persona que llama, los incrédulos dirán: "Este es un día difícil".

9.La gente de Nuh (Noé) negó (a su Mensajero) ante ellos, rechazaron a Nuestro esclavo y dijeron: "¡Un loco!" y fue reprendido y amenazado insolentemente.

10. Luego invocó a su Señor (diciendo): "¡He sido vencido, así que ayúdame!"

11. Entonces abrimos las puertas del cielo con agua a raudales.

12.E hicimos brotar manantiales de la tierra. Así que las aguas (del cielo y la tierra) se encontraron por un asunto predestinado.

13.Y lo llevamos en un (barco) hecho de tablas y clavos,

14. Flotando bajo Nuestros ojos, ¡una recompensa para el que había sido rechazado!

15.Y de hecho, hemos dejado esto como una señal, entonces, ¿hay alguien que recuerde (o reciba amonestación)?

dieciséis. Entonces, ¿qué tan (terrible) fue Mi Tormento y Mis Advertencias?

17.Y de hecho hemos hecho que el Corán sea fácil de entender y recordar, entonces, ¿hay alguno que recuerde (o reciba amonestación)?

18.'Ad (la gente) desmintió (a su Profeta, Hud), entonces, ¿qué tan (terrible) fue Mi Tormento y Mis Advertencias?

19. En verdad, enviamos contra ellos un viento furioso de voz áspera en un día de mal presagio y calamidad continua.

20. Arrancar a los hombres como si fueran tallos arrancados de palmeras datileras.

21. Entonces, ¿qué tan (terrible) fue Mi Tormento y Mis Advertencias?

22.Y de hecho hemos hecho que el Corán sea fácil de entender y recordar, entonces, ¿hay alguno que recuerde (o reciba amonestación)?

23.Thamud (la gente también) desmintió las advertencias.

24.Porque dijeron: "¡Un hombre! ¿Solo de entre nosotros, que vamos a seguir? ¡En verdad, entonces deberíamos estar en el error y la angustia o la locura! "

25."¿Es que el Recordatorio se le envía a él [el Profeta Salih (Saleh)] solo de entre nosotros? ¡No, es un mentiroso insolente! "

26.¡Mañana llegarán a saber, quién es el mentiroso, el insolente!

27.En verdad, les enviamos la camello como prueba. Así que obsérvalos [Oh Salih (Saleh)], ¡y ten paciencia!

28.E infórmeles que el agua se compartirá entre (ella y) ellos. Se establece el derecho de cada uno a beber (por turnos).

29.Pero llamaron a su camarada y él tomó (una espada) y la mató.

30. Entonces, ¿qué tan (terrible) fue Mi Tormento y Mis Advertencias?

31. En verdad, enviamos contra ellos un solo Saihah (tormento, grito terrible, etc.), y se volvieron como rastrojo seco de un constructor de pliegues.

32.Y de hecho, hemos hecho que el Corán sea fácil de entender y recordar, entonces, ¿hay alguno que recuerde (o reciba amonestación)?

33. La gente de Lout (Lot) desmintió las advertencias.

34. En verdad, enviamos contra ellos una violenta tormenta de piedras (que los destruyó a todos), menos a la familia de Lout (Lot), a quien salvamos en la última hora de la noche,

35. Como un favor nuestro, así recompensamos al que da gracias (obedeciéndonos).

36.Y él [Patán (Lot)] de hecho les había advertido de Nuestro Agarre, ¡pero ellos dudaban de las advertencias!

37.Y de hecho buscaron avergonzar a su invitado (pidiéndole que cometiera sodomía con ellos). Así que cegamos sus ojos, "Entonces prueba Mi Tormento y Mis Advertencias".

38.Y, en verdad, un tormento permanente se apoderó de ellos temprano en la mañana.

39."Entonces prueba Mi Tormento y Mis Advertencias".

40.Y de hecho, hemos hecho que el Corán sea fácil de entender y recordar, entonces, ¿hay alguno que recuerde (o reciba amonestación)?

41.Y de hecho, llegaron advertencias al pueblo de Fir'aun (Faraón) [a través de Musa (Moisés) y Harun (Aarón)].

42.(Ellos) desmintieron todos Nuestros Signos, así que los capturamos con un Asalto del Todopoderoso, Todopoderoso para llevar a cabo lo que Él quiera (Omnipotente).

43.¿Son tus incrédulos (¡oh, Quraish!) Mejores que estas [naciones de Nuh (Noé), Lout (Lot), Salih (Saleh) y la gente de Fir'aun (Faraón), etc., que fueron destruidos)? ¿O tienes inmunidad (contra Nuestro Tormento) en las Divinas Escrituras?

44.¿O dicen: "Somos una gran multitud, y saldremos victoriosos".

45. Su multitud huirá y mostrarán sus espaldas.

46. No, pero la Hora es su tiempo señalado (para su recompensa completa), y la Hora será más dolorosa y más amarga.

47. En verdad, los Mujrimun (politeístas, incrédulos, pecadores, criminales, etc.) están en el error (en este mundo) y arderán (en el fuego del Infierno en el Más Allá).

48. El día en que serán arrastrados en el fuego sobre sus caras (se les dirá): "¡Probad el toque del infierno!"

49. En verdad, hemos creado todas las cosas con Qadar (Preordenamientos divinos de todas las cosas antes de su creación, como está escrito en el Libro de Decretos Al-Lauh Al-Mahfuz).

50. Y Nuestro Mandamiento es solo uno, como un abrir y cerrar de ojos.

51. Y de hecho, hemos destruido tus gustos, entonces, ¿hay alguno que recuerde (o reciba amonestación)?

52. Y todo lo que han hecho se anota en (sus) Registros (de hechos).

53. Y todo, pequeño y grande, está escrito (en Al-Lauh Al-Mahfuz ya de antemano. Antes de que suceda, o lo haga su hacedor) (Ver el Corán V.57: 22).

54. En verdad, el Muttaqun (piadoso), estará en medio de Jardines y Ríos (Paraíso).

55. En un asiento de la verdad (el Paraíso), cerca del Rey Omnipotente (Alá, el Bendito, el Altísimo, el Dueño de la Majestad y el Honor).

Chapter 5 The Translation of Surah 54 Al-Qamar The Moon (La Luna) Spanish Version

VERSOS 1-8 EL DÍA DE la resurrección y la negligencia de los politeístas

Cuando el Profeta Muhammad entregó el mensaje de Dios a la gente de La Meca, la mayoría de ellos rechazó firmemente el concepto de resurrección. Ellos se negaron a aceptarlo como el Mensajero de Dios y exigieron que si este mundo realmente va a llegar a su fin, entonces debería haber alguna señal física, algún milagro que se les debería mostrar como prueba. Entonces, cinco años antes de la Hégira (migración) del Profeta a Medina,

Dios les hizo presenciar un milagro. Una noche vieron la luna dividida en dos pedazos y las dos mitades estaban tan separadas que cada una apareció a cada lado del monte Hira.

Después de un momento, la luna se volvió a unir. Uno pensaría que después de ver una señal tan tremenda, habrían aceptado la verdad, pero no afectó en absoluto su actitud. Ellos obstinadamente dijeron que era solo una especie de magia y nada más. ¿Por qué la gente persiste en permanecer ignorante de la verdad? ¿Por qué no aceptan pruebas tan claras? Es porque sus vidas giran en torno a sus propios deseos y su falsa autoimagen les hace casi imposible admitir que estaban persiguiendo ideales equivocados. Por eso, prefieren ignorar todas aquellas cosas que les incomodan al darse cuenta de la verdad.

La división de la luna no fue el único signo del poder de Dios; más bien, la gente de La Meca también estaba bien informada acerca de las naciones que habían sido destruidas antes que ellos, debido al rechazo del mensaje de Dios que los Profetas les habían traído.

Dios nos ha dado la opción de pensar y elegir nuestra forma de vida en este mundo, pero aquellos que hacen mal uso de esta opción y rechazan la guía de Dios no deben olvidar que llegará un día en que no podrán decir "no" a la llamador, quien los llamará hacia el Juicio final. Los discursos y argumentos arrogantes contra Dios y Su Profeta serán olvidados y se precipitarán ciegamente hacia su destino.

Versículos 9-42 El mal fue el fin de las naciones precedentes que desmentían a sus Mensajeros.

La gente de Noé era tan arrogante que olvidaron su propia impotencia. Dios envió sobre ellos una gran inundación que ahogó todo excepto la barca que llevaba al profeta Noé y las pocas personas que habían creído en Dios. Esto muestra la extrema misericordia y compasión de Dios por Su Mensajero y por los creyentes de la verdad, pero al mismo tiempo, Su castigo para aquellos que rechazan obstinadamente Su mensaje, también es evidente.

La gente de 'Ad era extremadamente poderosa, no solo en habilidades sino también en atributos físicos; pero cuando rechazaron continuamente el mensaje de Dios, les envió un viento muy frío que les dio un castigo humillante. Entonces la gente de Thamud también cometió el mismo error. También estaban muy orgullosos de su éxito en el mundo y pensaban que el Profeta Salih solo estaba difundiendo algunas historias o mentiras creadas por ellos mismos. Entonces exigieron un milagro y Dios les envió una camella, de la cual les habían advertido que no le hicieran ningún daño, pero la mataron pensando que podían salirse con la suya. En consecuencia, Dios les dio un final doloroso.

La gente de Lot fueron las primeras personas en entregarse a la homosexualidad, y había cegado sus sentidos hasta tal punto que cuando los ángeles llegaron a la casa del Profeta disfrazados de jóvenes, estas personas se apresuraron a tenerlos; nada les importaba excepto la satisfacción de su lujuria.

Lo mismo le sucedió al faraón, cuando se creyó indestructible.

Un malentendido común es que el Corán es para eruditos. Dios está diciendo con palabras tan claras que Él mismo nos ha facilitado la comprensión y ahora depende de nosotros contemplar y recibir su guía. Este es el único libro del mundo que ha sido leído por todo tipo de personas. Incluso las personas analfabetas pueden beneficiarse de su orientación clara. Junto con la simplicidad, hay una profundidad asombrosa en sus palabras que también estimula el intelecto de personas altamente instruidas.

Versos 43-55 Amenazando a los politeístas y dando buenas nuevas a los piadosos

¿Cómo pueden engañarse a sí mismos cuando Dios les ha enviado advertencias tan claras? Aquellos que persisten en su incredulidad y no se molestan en leer el Corán o seguir las enseñanzas del Profeta Muhammad, deben saber que están cometiendo un crimen terrible, incluso si tienen la ilusión de ser "buenas personas".

En este mundo, se burlaban de los creyentes porque les preocupaba demasiado el tormento del infierno. Su afirmación es que Dios es tan misericordioso que no puede quemar a nadie, pero Dios les advierte que este fuego definitivamente tocará a aquellos que se burlaron de él y no hicieron ningún esfuerzo por salvar sus almas de él.

Al final de este capítulo, Dios nos muestra un vistazo de los espléndidos jardines de las delicias, el hermoso Paraíso, que ha preparado con tanto amor para los que le han permanecido fieles en la vida mundana. Estas personas sacrificaron voluntariamente sus egos y deseos por la causa de Dios para que Él les dé esta maravillosa recompensa donde todos sus deseos se cumplirán eternamente.

References

Al-Kulayni, Abu Ja'far Muhammad ibn Ya'qub (2015). Kitab al-Kafi. South Huntington, NY: The Islamic Seminary Inc. ISBN 9780991430864.

Ibn Kathir. "Tafsir Ibn Kathir (English): Surah Al Qamar". Quran 4 U. Tafsir.

Ernst, Carl W., How to Read the Quran: A New Guide with Select Translations (Chapel Hill: The University of North Carolina Press, 2011).

Moon." In The Oxford Dictionary of Islam. edited by John L. Esposito. Oxford Islamic Studies Online,

Haleem, M.A.S. Abdel. The Quran (New York: Oxford University Press, 2005)

About the Author

"And give good tidings to those who believe and do righteous deeds that they will have gardens [in Jannah Paradise] beneath which rivers flow. Whenever they are provided with a provision of fruit therefrom, they will say, 'This is what we were provided with before.' And it is given to them in likeness. And they will have therein purified spouses, and they will abide therein eternally." (The Noble Quran 2:25)